世 界 文 化 遗 产

World Heritage

世界文化遺産

大足石刻

DAZU GROTTOES IN A NUTSHELL

中国旅游出版社
China Travel & Tourism Press

主　　编：王庆瑜
副 主 编：赵崇亮
摄　　影：王庆瑜　吕大千　龚威健
撰　　文：黎方银
英文翻译：胡志挥
地图编辑：孙素菊
责任编辑：吕大千
装帧设计：白志勇　乔加强

图书在版编目(CIP)数据

大足石刻／王庆瑜主编．—北京：中国旅游出版社，
2002.8
(旅游在中国)
ISBN 7-5032-2011-2

Ⅰ.大… Ⅱ.王… Ⅲ.大足石窟－石刻－摄影集
Ⅳ.K879.27-64

中国版本图书馆 CIP 数据核字 (2002) 第 049463 号

大足石刻

中国旅游出版社

地址：北京建国门内大街甲 9 号
邮政编码：100005　电话：65201010
北京中大彩视数码科技有限公司制版
深圳利丰雅高印刷有限公司印刷

2002 年 8 月第一版　第一次印刷
开本：850×1168 毫米　1/24　印张：4
印数：1—5000 册　中、英、日对照　005800

（版权所有　翻版必究）

辉煌的大足石刻

黎方银

大足石刻,始建于唐永徽元年(650),历经五代,盛于两宋,余绪延至明、清,是中国晚期石窟艺术的代表作品。

大足石刻,是重庆市大足县境内主要表现为摩崖造像的石窟艺术的总称。现公布为文物保护单位的摩崖造像,多达75处,雕像五万余身,铭文十万余字。其中,以北山、宝顶山、南山、石篆山、石门山摩崖造像最具特色。大足石刻于1999年12月1日,被联合国教科文组织作为文化遗产,列入《世界遗产名录》。

北山摩崖造像,位于大足县城龙岗镇北1.5千米处,开凿于唐景福元年(892)至南宋绍兴年间(1131~1162),通编为290号,造像近万尊,以其雕刻细腻、精美典雅著称于世,展示了晚唐至宋,中国民间佛教信仰及石窟艺术风格的发展、变化,被誉为唐宋石刻艺术陈列馆。

北山晚唐造像,端庄丰满,气质浑厚,衣纹细密,薄衣贴体,具有盛唐遗风。第5号毗沙门天王龛、第9号千手观音龛、第10号释迦牟尼佛龛、第51号三世佛龛、第52号阿弥陀佛龛等,是其代表作品。尤其是第245号观无量寿佛经变相,内容丰富,层次分明,刻有人物造像539身,各种器物460余件,保存了多方面的形象史料。在中国石窟同类题材造像中,首屈一指。

五代作品占北山造像的三分之一以上,是中国此期造像最多的地区,有着承上启下的重要作用。其特点是,小巧玲珑,体态多变,神情潇洒,纹饰渐趋繁丽,呈现出由唐至宋的过渡风格。如第53号的佛、菩萨像,既有唐代雕刻的丰满古朴,又具宋代造像的修长身躯。第273号的千手观音及其侍者,薄衣贴体颇具唐风,仪容秀丽又似宋刻。

北山宋代造像,以观音最为突出,被誉为"中国观音造像的陈列馆"。这一时期的作品,更加贴近生活,体现了宋代的审美情趣。造像,具有人物个性鲜明,体态优美,比例匀称,穿戴艳丽等特点。最具代表性的是第136号转轮经藏窟。该窟造像,以恬静的面部刻划反映其

内心之宁静,以玲珑的衣冠显其身份的高贵。以线造型,线面并重,富有中国民族特色。璎珞蔽体,飘带满身,花簇珠串,玲珑剔透,装饰味浓;且多保存完好,宛如新刻,被公认为是"中国石窟艺术皇冠上的一颗明珠"。其他,如第125号数珠手观音、第113号和第133号水月观音、第155号孔雀明王窟、第177号泗洲大圣龛、第180号十三观音变相窟等,都是此期的珍品。这些造像的形象、姿态、性格、神情,以至衣褶、饰物等,皆耐人寻味;组合变化丰富,刻工精美,步步移,面面观,出人意料的意境层出不穷。

宝顶山摩崖造像,位于大足县城东北15千米处,由宋代高僧赵智凤于南宋淳熙至淳祐年间(1174~1252),历时七十余年,以大佛湾、小佛湾为中心,有总体构思组织开凿而成,是一处造像逾万尊、在石窟中罕见的完备而有特色的大型佛教密宗道场,它把中国密宗史往后延续了400年左右,为中国佛教密宗史增添了新页。

宝顶山摩崖造像的表现形式,在石窟艺术中独树一帜。万余尊造像,题材不重复,龛窟间既有教义上的内在联系,又有形式上的相互衔接,形成一个有机的整体。其内容,始之以六趣唯心,终之以柳本尊正觉成佛,有教有理,有行有果,系统完备而有特色。

宝顶山摩崖造像,注重阐述哲理,把佛教的基本教义与中国儒家的伦理,理学的心性及道教的学说融为一体,兼采博收,显示了中国宋代佛学思想的特色。造像,既追求形式美,又注重内容的准确表达。其所显示的内容和宗教、生活哲理,对世人能晓之以理,动之以情,诱之以福乐,威之以祸苦。涵盖社会思想博大,令人省度人生,百看不厌。

宝顶山摩崖造像,以能慑服人心为其创作原则,借以激发信众对佛法的虔诚。造像、装饰、布局、排水、采光、支撑、透视等,都十分注重形式美和意境美。如千手观音1007只手,屈伸离合,参差错落,有如流光闪烁的孔雀开屏。释迦涅槃像,全长31米,只露半身,其构图有"意到笔伏,画外有画"之妙,给人以藏而不露之美感,这是中国山水画于有限中见无限这一传统美学思想的成功运用。地狱变相,刻有阴森恐怖的十八层地狱;牛头马面狰狞强悍,受罪人呼天号地;

尖刀、锯解、油锅、寒冰、沸汤诸般酷刑,惨不忍睹,令人触目惊心。圆觉洞内的数十身造像,刻工精细,衣衫如丝似绸,台座酷似木雕。洞口上方开一天窗采光,光线直射窟心,使洞内明暗相映,神秘莫测。九龙浴太子利用崖上的自然山泉,于崖壁上方刻九龙,导泉水至中央龙口而出,让涓涓清泉长年不断地洗涤着释迦太子,给造像平添了一派生机,堪称因地制宜的典范。

南山摩崖造像,开凿于南宋绍兴年间(1131~1162),通编为15号,是一处极其重要的道教造像区。如第5号三清古洞,共刻像421身,以道教最高神"三清"为主,配刻以"四御"及圣母、王母等群像,生动地反映了宋代道教神仙系统的演变过程。

石篆山摩崖造像,开凿于北宋元丰五年至绍圣元年(1082~1094),通编为10号,系典型的释、道、儒三教合一造像区。其中,第6号为孔子龛,正壁刻中国大思想家、儒家创始人孔子坐像,两侧壁刻十大弟子像。第7号为三身佛龛。第8号为老君龛,正中凿中国道教创始人老子坐像,左右各侍立7尊真人、法师像。

石门山摩崖造像,开凿于北宋绍圣元年至南宋绍兴二十一年(1094~1151),通编为16号,为佛教、道教合一造像区,尤以道教造像最具特色。如第2号玉皇大帝龛外的千里眼、顺风耳,筋脉显露,手法夸张。第7号独脚五通大帝,左脚独立于风火轮上,广额深目,袍带飞扬,有来去如风之势。第10号三皇洞造像,儒雅清秀,手法写实,人神合璧。第11号东岳大帝宝忏变相龛,以东岳大帝、淑明皇后居中,反映出宋代东岳世家在道教神系中的突出地位。

中国石窟艺术,在其长期的发展过程中,各个时期都积淀了自己独具特色的模式及内涵。以云冈石窟为代表的早期石窟艺术(魏晋时期,公元4~5世纪),受印度犍陀罗和笈多式艺术的影响较为明显,造像多呈现出"胡貌梵相"的特点。以龙门石窟为代表的中期石窟艺术(隋唐时期,公元6~9世纪),表现出印度文化与中国文化相融合的特点。作为晚期石窟艺术代表作的大足石刻,在吸收、融化前期石窟艺术精华的基础上,于题材选择、艺术形式、造型技巧、审美情趣诸方面,都较之

前代有所突破,以鲜明的民族化、生活化特色,成为具有中国风格的石窟艺术的典范,与敦煌、云冈、龙门等石窟一起,构成了一部完整的中国石窟艺术史。

大足石刻,题材多样,内容丰富,儒、释、道"三教"造像俱全,有别于前期石窟。以南山摩崖造像为代表的宋代道教造像,是中国这一时期雕刻最精美、神系最完备的道教造像群。石篆山摩崖造像中,以中国儒家创始人孔子为主尊的"儒家"造像,在石窟艺术中可谓凤毛麟角。以石篆山摩崖造像为代表的佛教、道教、儒教"三教"合一造像,以及以石门山摩崖造像为代表的佛教、道教合一造像,在中国石窟艺术中亦极为罕见。这些造像表明,宋代时期,"孔、老、释皆至圣","惩恶助善,同归于治"的"三教"合流的社会思潮已经巩固;世俗信仰对于"三教"的宗教界线,已日渐淡漠,呈现出信仰多元化的趋势。

大足石刻,对中国石窟艺术的创新与发展有重要贡献。它注重雕塑艺术自身的审美规律和形式规律,是洞窟造像向摩崖造像方向发展的佳例。在立体造型的技法上,运用写实与夸张互补的手法,摹难显之状,传难达之情,对不同的人物赋予不同的性格特征,务求传神写心。强调善恶、美丑的强烈对比,表现的内容贴近生活,文字通俗,达意简赅,既有很强的艺术感染力,又有着极大的社会教化作用。在选材上,既源于经典,而又不拘泥于经典,具有极大的包容性和创造性,处处反映出世俗信仰惩恶扬善、调伏心意和规范行为的义理要求。在布局上,是艺术、宗教、科学、自然的巧妙结合。在审美上,融神秘、自然、典雅三者于一体,充分体现了中国传统文化重鉴戒的审美要求。在表现上,突破一些宗教雕塑的旧程式,有了创造性的发展,神像人化,人神合一,极富中国特色。总之,大足石刻在诸多方面都开创了石窟艺术的新形式,成为具有中国风格和中国传统文化内涵,以及体现中国传统审美思想和审美情趣的石窟艺术的典范。

大足石刻,是石窟艺术生活化的典范。它以其浓厚的世俗信仰,纯朴的生活气息,在石窟艺术中独树一帜,把石窟艺术生活化推到了空前的境地。在内容取舍和表现手法

方面，都力求与世俗生活及审美情趣紧密结合。其人物形象文静温和，衣饰华丽，身少裸露；形体上，力求美而不妖，丽而不娇。造像中，无论是佛、菩萨，还是罗汉、金刚，以及各种侍者像，都颇似现实中各类人物的真实写照。特别是，宝顶山摩崖造像所反映的社会生活情景之广泛，几乎应有尽有，颇似一座宋代民间风俗画廊。无论王公大臣、官绅士庶、渔樵耕读，各类人物皆栩栩如生，呼之欲出，可以说是一幅生动的历史生活画卷，它从各个侧面浓缩地反映了晚唐至宋时期的中国社会生活，使源于印度的石窟艺术经过长期的发展，至此完成了中国化的进程。

总之，论其规模之大，造诣之精，内容之丰富，大足石刻都堪称是一项伟大的艺术杰作。它既是中国石窟艺术重要的组成部分，也是公元9世纪末至13世纪中叶，世界石窟艺术中最为壮丽辉煌的一页。

Splendid Dazu Grottoes

Written by Li Fangyin

Built continuously from the first year of the reign of Emperor Yonghui of the Tang Dynasty (650) to the Qing Dynasty, Dazu Grottoes are a beautiful gem in the treasure trove of grotto arts in China.

Located in Dazu County, 163 kilometres west of the city proper of Chongqing, the stone carvings of Dazu, chiefly consisting of Buddhist images, are the art of a religious nature. More than fifty thousand figure statues are scattered over seventy-five places. Those carved out of the rocks at Beishan, Baodingshan, Nanshan, Shizuanshan and Shimenshan are the most concentrated in number, the largest in scale, the finest in craftsmanship and the richest in content. In 1961 they appeared on the list of the first group of important cultural relics under state protection as announced by the State Council and in 1999 it was inscribed on the World Heritnge List by the UNESCO.

Situated 1.5 kilometres from the county seat of Dazu, the cliffside carvings at Beishan Mountain were generally accomplished during the late period

of Tang Dynasty and Five Dynasties (892-960), while those in the northern section were mainly carved in the Song Dynasty. Totaling nearly ten thousand pieces in number, these works are characterized with rotund and stately appearance, unsophisticated disposition and thin garments, reflecting the development and change of the common people's religious belief and the style of stone sculpture during the days from the late period of Tang Dynasty to the Song Dynasty.

The figures situated in the southern section of Fowan district were carved mainly during the late period of Tang Dynasty with the North Heavenly King (No.5), Thousand-arm Avalokitesvara (No. 9), Sakyamuni (No. 10), Trikala Buddhas (No. 51) and Amitabha (No. 52) as the representative works. Especially, in addition to excellent craftsmanship and wonderful arrangement, "A Scene of the Amitayus-Dhana-Sutra" (No. 245) is endowed with rich content. For instance, apart from having possessed 539 figure statues and 460 objects (including vessels and musical instruments), it has housed many valuable materials for the study of Chinese history. Hence, the value of this shrine comes first among the shrines with the same theme in Chinese grottoes.

The stone sculptures produced during the Five Dynasties cover nearly one third of the figure statues on Beishan Mountain. Besides, they played an important role in promoting the advance of Chinese grotto art.

Among Beishan cliffside carvings the most outstanding works are the statues of Avalokitesvara. The place is, therefore, reputed as "the Gallery of Avalokitesvaras". As an embodiment of the aesthetic standards peculiar to the artisans of the Song Dynasty, the images of figure statues produced in this period became more and more close to the reality of life. Endowed with distinct personalities, they have possessed the following common features: well-proportioned body; graceful manner; exquisitely dressed and easy posture. The most representative one of them is the image of Avalokitesvara with the Sun and Moon in No. 136 shrine. With ornament decorated on her breast, ribbons drifting gently over her body, this statue is portrayed in accordance with the Chinese aesthetic standards: plump face, small mouth, beautiful brows and eyes. Hence, it is acknowledged as a pearl on the crown of the Chinese grotto art. As outstanding works appearing in the same period of time, stone carvings such as Avalokitesvara with a Rosary (No. 125), Avalokitesvara Gazing at the Moon Reflection on Water (No. 113 and 133) and Peacock King (No. 155) are also rated as the art treasure of stone sculpture. Based on traditional skills, all of these figure statues are masterpieces regarding their harmonious unity between the line and the side, between the square and the round, and between the simple and the complex.

Baoding (Treasure Peak) Mountain, fifteen kilometres northeast of Dazu, is well-known for having housed more than ten thousand pieces of magnificent sculptures, which were created under the direction of a distinguished local Buddhist monk Zhao Zhifeng during the Southern Song Dynasty. Lasting for seventy-odd years, the construction was carried out mainly in the districts of Dafowan and Xiaofowan. Owing to the successful efforts of Monk Zhao, the history of the Esoteric Sect in China was thus able to continue for another four hundred years.

The artisans responsible for building the figure statues on Baoding Mountain paid great attention to elaborating the philosophic theory, making the fundamental doctrine of Buddhism mix together with the ethics of Confucianism, the rationalistic principles of Neo-Confucianism and the dogmas of Taoism. As a result, the special feature of Buddhism in China during the Song Dynasty lies in embracing all good points of various religious and academic schools.

With the intention of cowing the common people into submission, the construction of figure statues on Baoding Mountain is devoted to make the Buddhist followers become pious adherents by way of demonstrating the force of the Buddhist law. Therefore, in terms of design, decoration, layout, drainage, natural lighting, supporting and perspective, stress was usually laid on the beauty both in form and in imagination. For instance, the

statue of Thousand-Arm Avalokitesvara with actually 1007 arms in No. 8 shrine is about 3 metres in height . The arms, which cover an area of 88 square metres, stretch out just like the full display of a peacock's tail. All of her hands are different in gesture and look quite attractive and natural. Measuring 31 metres in length from head to knees, the statue of Sakyamuni in No. 11 shrine is, no doubt, an another good example to show that the artisans of ancient China were already good at applying the dialectical relationship between the limited and the unlimited, so the design of this shrine has left plenty room for visitors to give full play to their imagination. In the episode of 18 hells, many scenes were depicted to show the evil-doers' suffering from various kinds of punishment, such as climbing the hill planted with sharp knives; being put into the cauldron full of boiling oil; the freezing ice and the knee-chopping instrument. In the Cave of Full Enlightenment, the figure statues were ingeniously portrayed. The Bodhisattvas' robes look like real silk while their stone platforms seem just as same as carved in wood. Above the entrance to this shrine opens a large window, so the sunlight comes in and illuminates the grotto centre, making it look mysterious, deep and serene. In the Cave of Nine Dragons Bathing the Prince, having made use of a nearby spring, the sculptors carved nine dragons. As a result, the cool water was shedding from their mouth to bathe the newly-born Crown Prince. It is a good example of taking measures to suit local conditions.

The figure statues on Nanshan Mountain were carved mainly in the reign of Shaoxin during the Southern Song Dynasty (1131-1162). Consisting of 15 shrines in all, Nanshan is one of the important ritual sites to publicize the dogmas of Taoism. For instance, in the Cave of Taoist Trinity, 421 figure statues were carved. Accompanied by the "Four Deities", the Saint Mother and Queen Mother of the West, the "Trinity", the supreme masters of Taoism, were located in the centre of whole cave. This kind of arrangement reflects the change and development of Taoist god system in China.

The construction of cliffside carvings on Shizuanshan Mountain was carried out in the years from 1082 to 1096. Consisting of 10 shrines, Mt. Shizuanshan is a typical ritual site known for the co-existence of Buddhism, Taoism and Confucianism. Located in the 6th cave, the statue of Confucius, the great thinker of China, stands in the centre. On either side of this shrine line up the statues of his ten disciples. In the 7th cave sits the statue of Tripka Buddha. In the middle of the 8th cave situates the sitting statue of Laozi, the founder of Taoism, and on either side of his statue there line up seven statues of the Taoist true men and masters.

The project of cliffside carvings on Shimenshan Mountain was accomplished in the years from the reign of Shaozhi of the Northern Song Dynasty to the reign of Shaoxin of the Southern Song Dynasty (1094-1151). Consisting of 16 shrines, it is noted for having housed many attractive statues of Taoist deities. For instance, the statues of the Farsighted God and the Well-Informed God outside the shrine of Jade Emperor were carved in an exaggerative manner. The statue of One-Legged God in the 7th cave was quite extraordinary and impressive. The carvings in the Cave of Three Thrones were completed with a scholarly bearing. All these are a good example to present Buddhist figures as human beings. In the 'Story of God of Mt. Tai', the statues of the Mountain God and his wife were placed in the middle of this shrine, and this fact shows what an important position the aristocratic family of Mt. Tai has taken in the god system of Taoism.

In the long history of China's grotto art development, the early-stage grottoes with Yungang Grottoes as its representative were influenced by India's Grandhara and Gupta style. As a result, most of the figure statues produced during the early period (namely, in the years of the Wei and Jin Dynasties) bore an appearance close peculiar to either the Hus (the people living in the western region of China) or the Fans (i.e. Indians). However, among the works in Longmen Grottoes, the representative of the middle period of China's grotto art (i.e. in the years of the Sui and Tang

Dynasties, 6th-9th centuries), there emerged the feature of combining Chinese culture with Indian culture. As the representative of the late period of China's grotto art, Dazu Grottoes displayed the following fresh trend: on the basis of absorbing the experience accumulated by the masters of older generations, the artisans in Dazu succeeded in making a series of breakthroughs in the field of subject-matter choice, the form of art, the carving technique and the aesthetic standards. Endowed with a distinct feature of nationalization and secularization, Dazu Grottoes became finally a typical model of the grotto art with distinct style. Together with the achievement obtained in Dazu, Dunhuang, Yungang and Longmen, formed a splendid history of China's grotto art.

The cliffside carvings of Dazu are well-known for their variety in subject matter and richness in content, and their co-existence of Buddhism, Taoism and Confucianism. Nevertheless, they differ somewhat from the stone sculptures produced in the previous period. For instance, the figure statues of Taoist dieties on Nanshan Mountain appeared during the Song Dynasty, apart from being the most excellent works carved in this period of time, boast the first complete god system of Taoism. Among the cliffside carvings on Shizuanshan Mountain, stands a figure statue of Confucius, the founder of Confucianism. This is extremely rare in the history of Chinese grotto art. Meanwhile, the co-existence of Buddhism, Taoism and Confucianism in the construction of cliffside carvings on Shimenshan Mountain is also rarely seen in any other grottoes throughout China. It proves clearly that in the Song Dynasty Confucius, Laozi and Sakyamuni were all worshipped as Great Saints. In order to realize the common purpose of "punishing evil-doers and encourage people to do good", the ideological trend of combining Confucianism with Buddhism and Taoism was in the ascendant. With the disappearance of the demarcation line between the above-mentioned religious faiths, the pluralistic trend in the field of religious belief began to emerge.

The success of Dazu made a great

contribution to the further development of Chinese grotto art. Emphasizing on both the law of aesthetic standards and the law of art form, the outstanding practice in Dazu was regarded as a good example to promote the advance of the grotto art from cave chiselling to cliffside carving. In the field of technique to achieve three-dimensional effect, the artisans of Dazu were skilled in applying a method of combining realism with exaggeration. Besides, in order to make their works full of artistic appeal, they did their utmost to improve their means of presentation, including colour and language. In the choice of subject matter, instead of being a stickler for classics, they strove to take in all good points of their counterpart so as to blaze new trials. In terms of layout, they advocated the genious combination of art with religion and science. In the way of presentation, they broke through a set of fixed formula for the design of Buddhist figure statues, succeeding finally in presenting Buddhist figures as human beings and depicting scenes from everyday life. As a consequence, the artisans of Dazu Grottoes had opened up a brand new way by carving Buddhist statues with Chinese characteristics.

Different from earlier grottoes, Dazu Grottoes are acknowledged as the model to make group relief full of human touch. For instance, the group relief, such as "the Story from the Scripture on the Kindness of Parents", is none other than a neat epitome of practical social life during the Song Dynasty, which is rarely seen in any other part of China. In the choice of content and presentation, the artisans of Dazu Grottoes advocated combining the Buddhist world closely with the secular life. As a result, the cliffside carvings on Baodingshan Mountain cover a wide range of social background, and various characters, including sovereigns, high officials, gentry, scholars, fishermen, woodcutters and farmers, were all true-to-life. Just like a gallery of folk custom in the Song Dynasty, the stone sculptures in Dazu Grottoes not only reflect vividly the social life during the years from the late period of Tang Dynasty to the Song Dynasty, but also show clearly how the grotto art, which originated in India, began

to take root and flourish in China.

In short, in terms of either scale, attainment or rich storage, Dazu Grottoes can be rated as among the top masterpieces accomplished in the world. Apart from being an important component of China's grotto art, it is a glorious chapter in the history of world-wide grotto art during the years from the 9th to the 13th centuries.

光り輝く大足石刻

黎方銀

　大足石刻は中国晚期石窟芸術の代表作であり、開削が唐の永徽元年（650）に始まり、五代を経て両宋時代に最盛期を迎え、明・清時代までに続いた。

　大足石刻は重慶市大足県内にある、摩崖造象を主として表現する石窟芸術の総称である。現在までに75ヵ所以上の摩崖造象、5万体以上の彫像、10万字以上の銘文が文化財に指定されている。なかでも北山、宝頂山、南山、石篆山、石門山の摩崖造象は最も特色がある。大足石刻は1999年12月1日、国連のユネスコによって、名が世界遺産リストに書きいれられた。

　北山摩崖造象は大足県都の竜崗鎮北1.5kmの場所にあり、唐の景福元年—南宋の紹興31年（892-1162）に開削され、通号は第290号。1万体に近い造像は、彫刻の細密・典雅さと美しさをもって名が世に知られ、晚唐から宋までの中国民間における仏教信仰と石窟芸術風格の発展と変化を伝え、唐・宋時代石刻芸術の陳列品として褒め称えられている。

　北山の晚唐造像は、ふくよかで重々しく、気質が重厚である。薄くて体にぴったりした衣服は、紋様が細密で盛唐の遺風がある。第5号の毗沙門天王龕、第9号の千手観音龕、第10号の釈迦牟尼仏龕、第51号の三世仏龕、第52号の阿彌陀仏龕などはその代表作である。とくに第245号の観無量寿仏は、経変の内容が豊富で、各層の順序もはっきりで、539体の人物造像、460余点の各種器物が刻され、形態種類が揃い、中国の同類石刻造像の中においても屈指のものに数えられる。

北山地区は、造像の3分の1以上が五代時代の作品で、この時期の中国で造像が最も多い地区として、前を受け継ぎ後を開く重要な役割を持っている。その特徴は、こじんまりで体形の変化が多く、嬉しそうな表情をもち、紋飾も華麗で煩雑なように変化し、唐の宋への過渡期における風格を示した。たとえば第53号の仏像と菩薩像は、唐代彫刻の古朴さとふくよかさもあれば、宋代造像の細長い体躯も具えている。第273号の千手観音とそのじしゃは、薄くて体にぴったりした衣服を着て、唐代の風格に富んでいるが、秀麗な容儀はなんとなく宋代の作品に似通っている。

北山の宋代造像は観音が最も目立ち、中国観音造像の陳列室として誉れ高い。この時期の作品は、現実生活により接近し、宋代の美意識を示した。造像の人物は鮮明な個性を持ち、容姿が美しく服飾も華麗で、バランスがよく取れているなどの特徴がある。第136号の転輪経蔵窟はそのうちの代表である。この窟の造像は、落ち着いた顔立ちで静かな内心世界を表現し、色鮮やかな衣冠で高貴な身分を表し、線を持って形をつくり、線と面を同時に重視し、中国の民族特色に富んでいる。体全体は飄逸な隠銛、漂う衣帯、透き通った数珠などで飾られ、装飾の味わいが濃い。且つそのほとんどが完全な形に保たれ、中国石窟芸術の王冠に綴られた真珠として公認されている。ほかの例えば第125号の数珠手観音、第113号と第133号の水月観音、第155号の孔雀明王窟、第177号の胖洲代聖龕、第180号の十三観音変相窟などは、いずれもこの時期の逸品である。これらの造像は、容貌、姿勢、性格、表情、更には服飾まで、これもどれも人々に深く考えさせるものがある。組み合わせが変化に富み、彫刻工芸が精巧を極め、彫像の1つ1つに同じ物がなく、予想以外の意境は後を絶たない。

宝頂山摩崖造像は、大足県都東北15kmの場所にあり、宋代の趙智鳳高僧が南宋の淳熙年間から淳祐年間まで(1174-1252)、70余年がかりで、小仏湾と大仏湾を中心に、全体構想の下で組織して開削したもので、1万尊以上の造像をもつ大型仏教密宗道場である。その開削により、中国密宗の歴史が400年余り引き伸ばされ、中国仏教密宗史に新しい1ページが添えられた。

宝頂山摩崖造像は石窟芸術の表現形式において、我が独自の道を切り開いた。1万尊以上の造像に、題材が重複したものがなく、各龕窟間は教義上の内的連繋もあれば、形式上の相互接続もあり、完全な有機体を成している。内容は六趣唯心から正覚成仏まで、教理あり行果ありて、整ったシステムがある。

宝頂山摩崖造像は、哲理の釈明を重んじ、仏教の基本的な教義と中国儒家の論理、理学の心性と道教の学説を一体にもみ合って、中国宋代仏学思想の特色を示した。造像は形式美を求めながらも、内容の正確的な表現にも注意を払っている。示してくれた内容、宗教と生活の哲理などは、博大で社会にカバーし、人生への反省を呼び起こし、何回見ても厭きない。

宝頂山摩崖造像は説得力を創作の原則とし、これをもって信者の仏法に対する敬虔さを呼び起こす。造像、装飾、配置、排水、採光、補強支柱、透かし彫りなどは、形式美と意境美を考えて重視を払っている。たとえば千手観音の1007本の手は、卓曲したものあり、伸びたものあり、長短様々で宛も色鮮やかに広げた孔雀の尾羽のようである。長さ31mの釈迦涅槃像は、下半身を地下に隠し、構図には「画の外にまた画がある」といった妙があり、「隠して外に顕わさない」という中国山水画に見られる伝統的な美学思想をうまく運用している。地獄変相は、恐ろしい18層地獄、凶悪な牛頭馬面、悲痛のはなはだしい罪人などが刻され、剣の山、油の煮え立った鍋など様々な刑法を実施する場面は、惨たらしくて見るに忍びない。圓覚洞内の数10体の造像は、彫刻が細緻を極め、衣服が絹物のようで、台座が木彫りそのものそっくりである。洞の上方に採光のための天窓が開かれ、ここから射し込んできた明りにより、洞内は明くしたり暗くしたりして、いっそう神秘なように見えている。自然の泉を活用した九竜浴太子は、岩壁の上方に9匹の竜が刻まれ、竜の口を通して流れ落ちてくる清水は、年中絶え間なく沐浴中の太子の身に注いでいる。自然の手法を通して造像に生気を満たせたこの作は、場所の特徴を活用するモデルと言ってよい。

通号第15号の南山摩崖造像は、南宋紹興年間(1131-1162)に開削したもので、極めて重

要な仏教造像区である。例えば第5号の三清古洞は、合わせて421体の彫像のうち、道教で最も貴い三清を主とし、「四御」や聖母、王母なども彫られ、宋代道教諸神の系統変化を生き生きと反映している。

通号第10号の石篆山摩崖造像は、北宋の元豊5年―紹聖元年（1082-1096）に開削した、典型的な釈・道・儒三教合一の造像区である。そのうちの第6号の孔子龕は、正面に中国の大思想家で、儒教の創立者・孔子の座像が刻され、両側に彼の10人の弟子の影像が立っている。第7号は三身仏龕である。第8号の老君龕は、正面が中国道教の創立者・老子の座像で、左右両側にそれぞれ7人の真人と法師の造像が立つ。

通号第16号の石門摩崖造像は、北宋の紹聖元年から南宋の紹興21年（1094-1151）までの間に開削したもので、仏教・道教合一のこの造像区に、道教の造像は最も特色がある。例えば第2号の玉皇大帝龕外の千里眼と順風耳は、青筋を立たせるなど誇張的な手法が取り入れられた。第7号の独脚五通大帝は、左足が風火輪の上に立ち、広い額の下に眼がくぼみ、軽やかに風に靡いた衣帯は、大帝に風のように去来する勢いがあることを示唆している。写実の手法が取り入れた第10号の三皇洞は、造像が優雅で美しく、形態と表情とは立派に結びついている。第11号の東岳大帝宝巹変相龕は、東岳大帝と淑明皇后を真ん中に立たせることを持って、道教諸神における宋代東岳世家の目立った地位を反映している。

中国の石窟芸術は長い発展期に、各時期にもそれぞれ異なった特色、パターンと内容を創り出した。雲崗石窟を代表とする早期（魏晋時期、西暦4-5世紀）石窟芸術は、インドの犍陀羅と笈式芸術からの影響が比較的に目立ち、造像には「胡貌頤相」（インド人顔立ちの胡人）の特徴が多く見られた。竜門石窟を代表とする中期（邉唐時期、西暦6-9世紀）石窟芸術は、インド文化に中国文化を融け込ませた特徴が見られた。晩期石窟芸術の代表作としての大足石刻は、前期石窟芸術の精華を吸収して消化したことを基礎に、題材選択、芸術形式、造形技巧、美意識など各方面において、前代と比べて打ち破ったことがあり、鮮明な民族的、生活的特色をもって、中国風格の

ある石窟芸術のモデルと成り、敦煌、雲崗、竜門各地の石窟とともに、完全な中国石窟芸術史を構成している。

大足石刻は、題材が多様で、豊富な内容を持ち、儒・釈・道三教の造像を揃え、前期石窟とは区別がある。南山摩崖造像を代表とする宋代道教造像は、この時期中国で彫刻が最も美しく、諸神系統を最も完全に揃えた道教造像群である。石篆山摩崖造像の中の、中国儒家学派の創立者・孔子を主像とする「儒家」造像は、石窟芸術においては希にしか見ないものと言えよう。石篆山摩崖造像を代表とする仏教・道教・儒教三教合一の造像、および石門山摩崖造像を代表とする仏教・道教合一の造像は、中国石窟芸術の中においても極めてまれなものである。これらの造像は、宋代に「孔子、老子、釈迦は皆、至聖なり」、「悪を懲らしめ善を助け、ともに治に帰す」などの「三教」合流の思潮がすでに固められ、世俗の「三教」に対する信仰が日に日に薄くなり、信仰多元化の趨勢が現われたことを物語っている。

大足石刻は中国石刻芸術の創新と発展に重要な貢献をした。彫塑芸術自身の審美眼と形式の表現規律を重視する大足石刻は、洞窟造像が摩崖造像に発展した素晴らしい一例である。立体造形の技法における、表現し難いところを表現し、様々な人物にそれぞれ異なった性格を持たせ、真実の心理内部を描き、善悪・美醜の強烈なコントラストを強調し、表現したい内容を生活に接近させるという写実と誇張を互いに補足し合うその運用手法は、つくりが簡単だが意味が深く、芸術的感染力が強く、社会に対して極めて大きな教育的・感化的役割を果たした。題材は、経典に取材したものが多いが、経典に拘泥せず、極めて大きな内包性と創造性を具え、悪を懲らしめ善を高揚させ、心意と行為を調和するという世俗の信仰をところどころ反映している。配置は芸術、宗教、科学と自然を巧みに結びついている。審美眼の面においては、神秘、自然と典雅を一身に溶け合って、鑑戒を重んじるという中国の伝統文化に要求された美意識を十分に示している。表現の面にあたっては、一部の宗教彫塑の古い枠を打ち破って創造的に発展させ、神を人間化させ、人・神を一身に集めるなど中国の

特色に富んでいる。総じて言えば、大足石刻は様々な方面で、石窟芸術の新しい形式を切り開き、中国の風格と中国の文化内容を具えて、中国の伝統的な美意識を具現する石窟芸術のモデルと成った。

　大足石刻は石窟芸術生活化のモデルと言ってよく、濃厚な世俗信仰と純朴な生活の息吹をもって、石窟芸術において我が独自の旗印を打ち建てて、石窟芸術の生活化をこれまでになかった境地に推し広めた。内容の取り捨てと表現手法の面では、世俗生活と審美眼との完全な結合にできる限り力を入れた。人物の造形が温和で落ち着き、全身が豪華な服飾で飾られ、露わにしたものが少なく、体形の美を求めながらも度を過ぎなく、仏も菩薩も羅漢も金剛も、さらにじしゃでさえすべては現実生活の人物そのもののようで真実である。とくに宝頂山摩崖造像は、反映した社会生活の情景が幅広く、あるべきものがすべてあり、王族、大臣、官僚、漁民、農夫、書生など各種人物が呼べば歩き出すのようで生き生きと刻され、晩唐から宋までの社会生活をまとめて様々な側面から反映し、宛も宋代の民間風俗画廊のようである。インドに源を持つ石窟芸術は長期にわたる発展をへて、中国化の道程がこれで終わったのである。

　総じて言えば、大足石刻は規模が大きく、つくりが素晴らしく、内容が豊富で、偉大な芸術傑作と言っても過言でない。大足石刻は、中国石窟芸術の重要な一構成部分であると同時に、また紀元9世紀末から13世紀中葉までの、世界石窟芸術史の最も燦爛たる1ページである。

玉印观音头像

Avalokitesvara with Jade Seal

玉印観音頭像

释迦涅槃圣迹图—宝顶山第11号 南宋

Sculptures showing Sakyamuni entering Nirvana
(No. 11, Baodingshan, Southern Song)

釈迦涅槃聖跡図——宝頂山第11号 南宋

　　释迦牟尼是佛教的创始人。涅槃是佛教宣扬的"不生不死,常乐我净"的最高境界。此涅槃像长达31米,头北脚南,背东面西,右侧横卧,下半身隐入崖际,右肩陷于地下,仅现大半个身躯,有"意到笔伏,画外有画"之妙,给人以藏而不露之美感。佛前弟子,似从地涌出,垂眉致哀;龛顶佛母眷属,手捧供物,面露悲恸之情。整组造像,虚实相济,气势宏大,意境深邃,既合仪轨,又有创新,为中国石窟艺术群中罕见。

　　Sakyamuni is the founder of Buddhism. To show the sacredness and greatness of Sakyamuni Buddha, only the upper part of body was chiselled, and thus leaving plenty room for visitors' imagination of the lower part. Located in the eastern cliff of Dafowan, the grand statue measures 31 metres in length from head to knees. With his eyes half closed, his head northwards, Sakyamuni lies on his right side which seems to sink into the ground. His disciples line up before him and lament the Buddha sadly while his mother, aunt and wife appear with the burning joss sticks in their hands. As excellent works of the Chinese stone sculpture, this group of carvings display a magnificent and splendid scene of Sakyamuni Entering Nirvana.

　　釈迦牟尼は仏教の創立者である。涅槃とは、仏教が宣揚する「不生不死、常楽我浄」の最高境地である。釈迦涅槃像は長さが31mに達し、頭を北において足を南に向け、東を背にして西に面し、右肩側を斜めにして横になっている。下半身と右肩が岩に隠れて、体の大半しか露出せず、「画の外に画があり、隠して顕わさない」といった妙を見る人に与えてくれる。地下から出てきたかのような弟子たちは、涙を流して哀れみ、龕上の仏母や家族は供物を手にして、悲しみを顔に顕わす。造像全体は虚あり実ありて、気勢が雄大で意味が深く、仕来りに合いながらも創新したことがあり、中国石窟芸術のごく希な逸品である。

14

(第14页图片说明)
观无量寿佛经变相——宝顶山第18号 南宋

A scene of the Amitayus-Dhana-Sutra
(No. 18, Baodingshan, Southern Song)

(14ページの写真説明)
観無量寿仏経変相——宝頂山第18号 南宋

(第16页图片说明)
大方便佛报恩经变相——宝顶山第17号 南宋

Three Saints of the Avatamsake School
(No. 5, Baodingshan, Southern Song)

(16ページの写真説明)
大方便仏報恩経変相——宝頂山第17号 南宋

(第18页图片说明)
地狱变相——宝顶山第20号 南宋

The Episode of 18 Hells
(No. 20, Baodingshan, Southern Song)

(18ページの写真説明)
地獄変相——宝頂山第20号 南宋

柳本尊行化事迹图——宝顶山第21号 南宋

Master Liu's Religious Centre
(No. 21, Mount Baoding,, Southern Song)
Liu Benzun, a master monk of the Southern song dynasty,is known for his ten practices of asceticism.

柳本尊行化事跡図——宝頂山第21号 南宋

六道轮回图——宝顶山第 3 号 南宋

Image of Six Ways of Transmigration
(No. 3, Baodingshan, Southern Song)

六道輪回図——宝頂山第 3 号 南宋

图中无常大鬼长舒两臂抱"六趣轮"。该轮是佛教"因果报应"、"轮回转世"、"十二因缘"、"善恶殊报"教义的形象体现。中国石窟群中刻六道轮回图者仅此一铺。

With a giant ghost getting his arms around the Buddhist wheel, the Image of Six Ways of Transmigration is none other than a vivid explanation of many Buddhist doctrine, such as "Twelve Predestined Relationship", "Retribution Justice", "Transmigration and Reincarnation". It is the first of its kind in the history of Chinese stone carvings.

図中の無常大鬼が両手を広げて「六趣輪」を抱いている。六趣輪は仏教の教義、「因果報応、輪回転世、十二因縁、善悪殊報」の形象化されたものである。中国で六道輪回図が刻された石窟はこれしかない。

护法神像——宝顶山第2号 南宋

Guardians of Buddhist Law
(No. 2, Baodingshan, Southern Song)

護法神像——宝頂山第2号　南宋

护法神即护卫佛法之神，为佛和菩萨之降魔化身。佛教称佛和菩萨为觉醒众生，为其摧毁魔障，故现愤怒像。

In order to enlighten all living creatures and to exorcise evil spirits, the image of Dharma Protector in Buddhism was usually carved with an angry expression.

護法神とは仏法を護る神のことで、仏と菩薩が降生して悪魔化したものである。仏教では仏と菩薩を覚醒衆生と呼び、悪魔を取り残す魔であるため、怒った顔つきになっている。

华严三圣像局部——宝顶山第5号 南宋

Three Saints of the Avatamsake School
(No. 5, Baodingshan, Southern Song)

華厳三聖像局部——宝頂山第5号 南宋

(第24页图片说明)
华严三圣像——宝顶山第5号 南宋

　　中为毗卢遮那佛，左右为文殊、普贤，合称"华严三圣"。三圣像依崖屹立，身向前倾，成功地避免了透视变形；袈裟绉褶舒展，披肩挂肘，直至脚下，支撑手臂，使文殊手中所托数百斤重的石塔历千年而不下坠。

Three Saints of the Avatamsake School
(No. 5, Baodingshan, Southern Song)

Vairocana sits in the middle, with Manjusri on the left side and Pushan Samantabhadra on the right side. They are collectively known as Three Saints of the Avatamsake School. It is due to the excellent design of their arrangement, the large pagoda on Manjusri's palm which weighs more than one hundred catties, remains as steady as before though it was carved one thousand years ago.

(24ページの写真説明)
華厳三聖像——宝頂山第5号 南宋

真ん中は毗盧遮那仏で、左右両側の文殊、普賢とともに「華厳三聖」と併称される。崖壁に寄りかかって彫られ、やや前に傾けた胴体は、透視によって引き起こされる変形をうまく避けている。軽やかに肩の上に掛けられた袈裟は、膝まで垂れて両手を支え、文殊の手に持った重さ数百kgの石塔が千年経っても落ちてこないように固めている。

千手观音像——宝顶山第8号 南宋

**Head of Thousand-Arm Avalokitesvara
(No. 8, Baodinghshan, Southern Song)**

千手観音像——宝頂山第8号 南宋

造型艺术中的千手观音多为32只手或48只手。而此观音像占崖88平方米，有1007只手、眼。千手或托宝塔，或执兵器，或握工具，或持乐器，或拿文房四宝，或捧宝珠法物等；其姿或伸、或曲、或正、或侧，形若流星闪烁，状如孔雀开屏，被誉为"天下奇观"。

The sitting statue of Avalokitesvara was carved with 1007 arms which cover an area of 88 square meters and stretches out like the tail of a peacock in full display. The hands are different in gesture and seem rather natural. This statue claims to be a wonder in the world.

観音の芸術造像は、手が32本か48本のものが多い。88m²の岩壁面積を占めたこの千手観音造像は、1007本の手と眼をもっている。曲がったり伸びたりした1本1本の手は、宝塔や兵器または道具、楽器、文房四宝、法物を持っている。全体は宛も美しく広げた孔雀の尾羽のようで、天下の奇観と絶賛されている。

27

父母恩重经变相龛——宝顶山第15号 南宋

Sculptures of Parental Love Sutra
(No. 15, Baodingshan, Southern Song)

父母恩重経変龕——宝頂山第15号 南宋

　　此龛造像以宣扬父母养育子女的辛劳为主题，以"佛前求子"为序，图文并茂地刻出"怀胎守护"、"临产受苦"、"生子忘忧"、"哺乳不尽"、"咽苦吐甘"、"推干就湿"、"远行忆念"等10组雕像。情节连贯，形象生动，感人肺腑，是一幅生动的世俗家庭生活图。寓中国儒家伦理于佛教义范之中，生动地体现了儒家的孝道思想，这在前期石窟造像中极其罕见。

　　The shrine is 7 meters high and 14 meters wide. In the lower tier there are the pictures devoted to describe the parental love. Consisting of ten episodes, the most vivid and minute of them are: "Pregnancy Care," "The Pangs of Parturition", "Nursing a baby" and "Mother's Preferring the Wet to Dry When Baby Making Sudden Water at Night". These episodes describe the parental love. Obviously, the content is laced with Confucianism. This group of carvings proves that the religious art began to become secularization after it was infiltrated by Confucianism. Such an arrangement is rarely seen in any other grottoes throughout China.

　　子女を養育する父母の辛苦をテーマとする造像である。「仏前子を求める」を序幕とし、「懐妊時の注意」、「産前の苦しみ」、「子を得た喜び」、「尽きない哺乳」をはじめ10組の彫像からなっている。物語としての前後の筋がつづき、造形が生き生きとしていて真に迫り、見る人を深く感動させる世俗家庭生活図と言ってよい。仏教教義に中国の儒家論理を融けこませて、儒家の孝道思想を生き生きと表現したこの龕の造像は、前期石窟造像においては、極めて希である。

(第30页图片说明)
临产受苦——宝顶山第15号 南宋

"Pangs of Parturition"
(No. 15, Baodingshan, Southern Song)

(30ページの写真説明)
産前の苦しみ——宝頂山第15号 南宋

谆谆教诲——宝顶山第15号 南宋

Instructing Earnestly and Tirelessly
(No. 15, Baodingshan, Southern Song)

くれぐれも言い聞かせて教える——宝頂山第15号 南宋

(第32页图片说明)
咽苦吐甘——宝顶山第15号 南宋

Nursing a baby
(No. 15, Baodingshan, Southern Song)

(32ページの写真説明)
苦しみ後の楽しみ——宝頂山第15号 南宋

生子忘忧——宝顶山第15号 南宋

The birth of a baby brought joy to the farmily
(No. 15, Baodingshan, Southern Song)

子を得た喜び——宝頂山第15号 南宋

推干就湿——宝顶山第15号 南宋

Preferring the wet to the dry
(No. 15, Baodingshan, Southern Song)

湿を干に取り替える——宝頂山第15号

并肩耳语——宝顶山第 30 号 南宋

Whispering
(No. 30, Baodingshan, Southern Song)

肩を並べてささやく——宝頂山第 30 号 南宋

(第38页图片说明)
吹笛女——宝顶山第17号 南宋

Flute-blowing girl
(No. 17, Baodingshan, Southern Song)

(38ページの写真説明)
笛吹く女——宝頂山大17号　南宋

养鸡女——宝顶山第20号 南宋

A hen-feeding woman
(No. 20, Baodingshan, Southern Song)

鶏飼女——宝頂山第20号　南宋

大方便佛报恩经变相——宝顶山第17号 南宋

Sakyamuni's filial piety
(No. 17, Baodingshan, Southern Song)

大方便仏報恩経変相——宝頂山第17号 南宋

(第40页图片说明)图正中刻释迦佛半身巨像,左右壁图文并茂地刻出释迦"亲探父王病"、"亲担父王棺"、"割肉供父母"、"舍身饲虎"、"剜眼出髓为父王治病"、"鹦鹉行孝"等因地修行、行孝,以及"六师外道谤佛不孝"等12组雕像。内容丰富,场面恢宏,雕像生动。

  The statue of Sakyamuni is located in the middle. Consisting of twelve episodes, the serial story depictshis filial piety in his present and previous lives, including "At the burial service for his deceased father, he personally carries the coffin together with the others", "To nourish his parents, he cuts off a slice of his own flesh", "When his father falls ill, he offers one of his own eyes as a medicine" and "The six heretics who made a slander on his unfilial conduct".

(40 ページの写真説明)
  岩壁の真ん中はお釈迦さまの巨大な半身像が彫られ、左右の両側は「自ら父の看病をする」、「自ら父の棺を担ぎ」、「我が身の肉を割って父母に供する」、「我が身を虎の餌にする」、「父の疾病を治療するためにわが眼と骨髄を取り出す」、「親孝行をするオウム」など親孝行を宣揚する*12 組の影像*が彫られている。場面が大きくて彫像の数々が生き生きとして真に迫り、内容も豊富である。

（第42页图片说明）
拍板人和舞蹈者——宝顶山第17号　南宋

The man playing bamboo clapper and A male dancer
(No. 17, Baodingshan, Southern Song)

(42ページの写真説明)
拍子木をたたく人——宝頂山第17号　南宋

大孝释迦佛亲担父王棺——宝顶山第17号南宋

At the burial service for his deceased father, Sakyamuni
personally carries the coffin together
with the others.(No.17, Baodingshan, Southern Song)

自ら父親の棺を担ぐお釈迦様——宝頂山第17号　南宋

观无量寿佛经变相——宝顶山第18号 南宋

A scene of the Amitayus-Dhana-Sutra
(No. 18, Baodingshan, Southern Song)

観無量寿仏経変相——宝頂山第18号 南宋

　　此龛造像上部刻"西方极乐净土"盛况。正中为阿弥陀佛、观音、大势至菩萨,合称"西方三圣"。下部及其左右分别刻"三品九生"、莲花化身童子和"十六观"图像等。其间引人注目的是信女、荷花童子及乐童等像。全图规模之大,堪称中国石窟艺术同类题材造像之最。

Consisting of more than 30 groups of stone sculptures, this shrine is devoted to depicting "the Pure Land of West". A bust of Amitabha stands in the middle, with the Goddess of Mercy on his right and Bodhisattva Mahasthama on his left. Pavilions and garrets erect on the uper tier and, on either side of the lower tier, there line up the statues and pictures, such as "Nine Ranks of Celestials"and "the Story of 16 Meditations", of which the most attractive are the images of female Buddhist followers, kids sitting on lotus and boy musicians. Due to its grand scale, this shrine is regarded as the most magnificent one in the history of Chinese grottoes.

　　この龕の上部は西方極楽浄土の盛況ぶりが彫られ、真ん中は阿弥陀仏、観音、大勢至菩薩で、西方三聖と併称される。下部と左右両側はそれぞれ「三品九生」、「蓮華化身童子」と「十六観」などが彫られている。なかでも信女、蓮華童子と楽童像はとくに人々の目を引く。雄大な規模のこの造像は、中国同類題材の石窟芸術のトップと言ってよい。

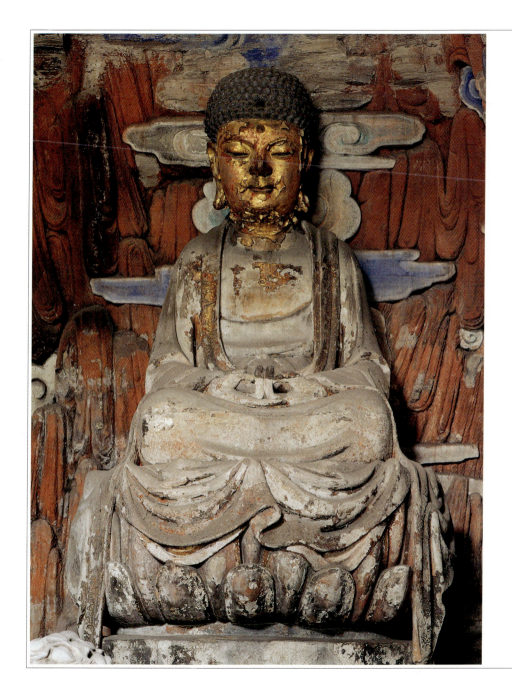

(第46页图片说明)
迦陵频伽——宝顶山第18号 南宋

Flying Celestial (Kalavinka)
(No. 18, Baodingshan, Southern Song)

(46 ページの写真説明)
迦陵頻伽——宝頂山第18号 南宋

卢舍那佛坐像——宝顶山第29号 南宋

The statue of sitting Buddha (Vairocana)
(No, 29 Baodingshan, Southern Song)

盧舎那仏坐像——宝頂山第29号 南宋

乐童——宝顶山第18号 南宋

One of the boy musicians
(No. 18, Baodingshan, Southern Song)

楽童——宝頂山第18号 南宋

乐童——宝顶山第18号 南宋

One of the boy musicians
(No. 18, Baodingshan, Southern Song)

楽童——宝頂山第18号 南宋

50

(第50页图片说明)
大宝楼阁——宝顶山第18号 南宋

Pavilion of Extensive Treasures
(No. 18, Baodingshan, Southern Song)

(50ページの写真説明)
大宝楼閣——宝頂山第18号 南宋

武士像——宝顶山第18号 南宋

Sculpture of a warrior
(No. 18, Baodingshan, Southern Song)

武士像——宝頂山第18号 南宋

（第52页图片说明）
地藏菩萨——宝顶山第20号 南宋

Ksitigarbha Bodhisattva
(No. 20, Baodingshan, Southern Song)

(52ページの写真説明)
地蔵菩薩——宝頂山第20号 南宋

铁轮地狱——宝顶山第20号 南宋

Hell of Iron Wheel
(No. 20, Baodingshan, Southern Song)

鉄輪地獄——宝頂山第20号 南宋

粪秽地狱——宝顶山第20号 南宋

Hell of Dirt ant Filth
(No. 20, Baodingshan, Southern Song)

糞穢地獄——宝頂山第20号 南宋

(第54页图片说明)

寒冰地狱——宝顶山第20号 南宋

Hell of Freezing Ice
(No. 20, Baodingshan, Southern Song)

(54ページの写真説明)
寒冰地獄——宝頂山第20号 南宋

油锅地狱——宝顶山第20号 南宋

Hell of Cauldron Full of Boiling Oil
(No. 20, Baodingshan, Southern Song)

油鍋地獄——宝頂山第20号 南宋

十王侍者之一——宝顶山第 20 号 南宋

An attendent to Yama
(No. 20, Baodingshan, Southern Song)

十王侍者之一——宝顶山第 20 号 南宋

十王侍者之二——宝顶山第 20 号 南宋

An attendent to Yama
(No. 20, Baodingshan, Southern Song)

十王侍者之二——宝顶山第 20 号 南宋

十王侍者之三——宝顶山第 20 号 南宋

An attendent to Yama
(No. 20, Baodingshan, Southern Song)

十王侍者之四——宝顶山第 20 号 南宋

An attendent to Yama
(No. 20, Baodingshan, Southern Song)

58

截膝地狱——宝顶山第20号 南宋

Hell of Knee-Chopping
(No. 20, Baodingshan, Southern Song)

截膝地獄——宝頂山第20号 南宋

  该地狱是佛教十八层地狱之一。佛教认为，饮酒乱性，故应戒酒；凡饮酒与劝人饮酒者，当下此地狱。全图刻酒后父子、兄弟、夫妻、姊妹相互不识，以及因卖酒、劝人饮酒、酒后乱伦常，死后皆入"地狱"等情景，绘声绘色地将中国宋代街巷酒肆的喧嚣之情凝固于石壁之上。

  Hell of Knee-Chopping is one the 18 hells. According to the doctrine of Buddhism, drinking should be forbidden since drunkards might do something immoral, and those who are fond of liquor and those who advise others to drink wine must be punished by chopping their knees off in the Hell. This group of carvings presents nine pictures including "Wine seller". "A husband failing to recognize his wife" "A man failing to recognize his son" and "Knee-chopping punishment". It is, in fact, a vivid description of the local life during the Song dynasty.

  截膝地獄は仏教が宣揚する十八層地獄の1つ。仏教は飲酒を乱性として禁酒をする。飲酒または他人に酒を勧める人は、地獄に行かされる。彫像群は、飲酒後の親子、兄弟、夫妻、姉妹が互いに見知らず、酒を売った人、他人に酒を勧めた人、飲酒後に乱倫した人は、死後いずれも地獄に行かされるなどを表現して、中国宋代街角の酒屋の情景を生き生きと岩壁に彫っている。

杀父淫母——宝顶山第20号 南宋

Two drunkards-one sexually harasses his mother,
the other kills his father
(No. 20, Baodinshan, Southern Song)

殺父淫母——寶頂山第20号 南宋

夫妻不识——宝顶山第20号 南宋

Drunken husband failing to recognize his wife
(No. 20, Baodingshan, Southern Song)

夫 妻知らず——宝顶山第20号 南宋

姐妹不识——宝顶山第 20 号 南宋

Drunkun elder sister failing to recognize the younger one
(No. 20, Baodingshan, Southern Song)

姉 妹知らず——宝頂山第 20 号 南宋

(第 63 页图片说明)
地狱变老年夫妇像——宝顶山第 20 号 南宋

An aged couple and their child
(No. 20, Baodingshan, Southern Song)

(63 ページの写真説明)
地獄変老年夫婦像——宝頂山第 20 号 南宋

十大明王像——宝顶山第22号 南宋

Statues of ten great Vidyarajas
(No. 22, Baodingshan, Southern Song)

十大明王像——宝顶山第22号 南宋

　　明王是指佛、菩萨受大日如来教令,降伏诸恶魔时变现出的威猛愤怒形象。作为十大明王之实例,目前中国仅见于此。中国当代著名雕塑大师刘开渠先生认为,此处的愤怒明王可与大卫像媲美。

　　It is believed in Buddhism that the ten Vidyarajas are designated to exorcise evil spirits. In such a case, they all put on an awe-inspiring look. Just as remarked by Liu Kaiju, a well-known Chinese sculptor , the statues of Vidyarajas in Irritation claim to be a match to "David" by Michelangelo.

　　明王とは、仏や菩薩が大日如来の令を受けて、諸悪魔を降服するために見せた獰猛な容貌のことを指す。現在中国に残った十大明王の実例はこれしかない。中国の現代彫塑大家の劉開渠先生は、この憤怒明王はダウィードに匹敵する美しさがあるとしている。

火明王——宝顶山第22号 南宋

Vidyarajas with a fith head
(No. 22, Baodingshan, Southern Song)

火明王——宝顶山第22号 南宋

降三世明王——宝顶山第22号 南宋
Worldly Evil-Subduing Vidyarajas
(No. 22, Baodingshan, Southern Song)
降三世明王——宝顶山第22号 南宋

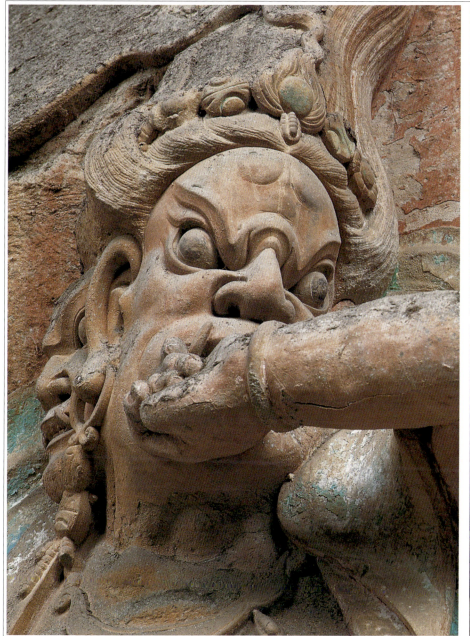

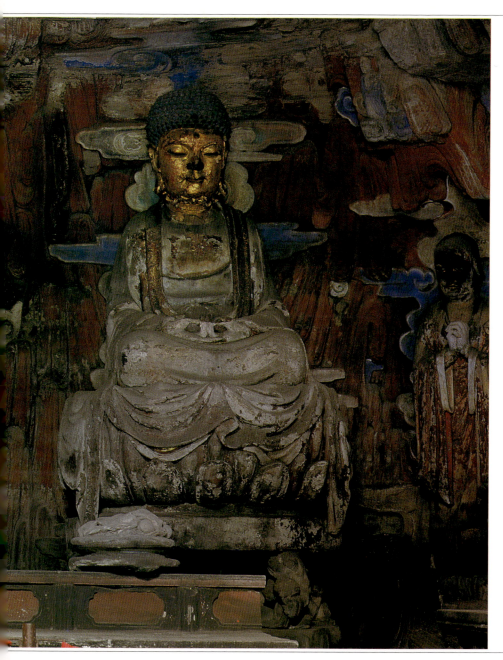

圆觉洞—宝顶山第29号 南宋

Cave of Full Enlightenment
(No. 29, Baodingshan, Southern Song)

円覚洞——宝頂山第29号 南宋

"圆觉"是菩萨修行功德圆满之意。洞内数十身造像刻工精细，衣衫如丝似绸，台座酷似木雕。洞口上方开一天窗采光，光线直射窟心，使洞内明暗相映，神秘莫测，充分展现出古代雕刻大师善造典型环境的才能。

The grotto is 6 meters high, 9 meters wide and 12 meters deep. Three Buddhas are sitting against the back wall of the grotto. Twelve Bodhisattvas, including Manjusri and Samantabhadra are sitting with free posture along the right and left walls. Right in the middle of the grotto a Bodhisattva figure is kneeing before the Buddha. All the statues appear solemn and respectful. Their robes look like real silk. The stone platforms look exactly like a product carved in wood. Above the entrance to this grotto opens a large window. As a result, light comes through it, illuminating the grotto center and making it mysterious, deep and serene. It shows clearly that Chinese ancient artisans had mastered a high skill in accomplishing stone sculptures according to their concrete enviroment.

円覚とは、菩薩の修行が円満に達したことの意味である。洞内数十体の造像は、つくりが繊細で、衣服が絹かシルクと思わせ、台座が木彫りそのものそっくである。洞の上方に採光のための天窓が開かれ、ここから射し込んできた明りにより、洞内は明くしたり暗くしたりして、いっそう神秘なように見えている。古代の彫刻大家が典型環境の創り出しに長けていること十分に示している。

圆觉洞右壁——宝顶山第29号 南宋
The right wall in the Cave of Full Enlightenment
(No. 29, Baodingshan, Southern Song)

(第75页图片说明)
三清像——南山第5号 南宋

Statues of the Taoist Trinity
(No.5, Nanshan, Southern Song)

(75ページの写真説明)
三清像——南山第5号 南宋

侍者像——南山第5号 南宋

Attendants (No.5, Nanshan, Southern Song)

侍者像——南山第5号 南宋

老君龛——石篆山第8号 北宋

The Niche of Laozi
(No. 8, Shizuanshan, Northern Song)

老君龛——石篆山第 8 号 北宋

阿修罗战帝释天故事图局部
——石门山第8号 南宋

Axiulo fighting against Sovereign Sakra (Partial)
(No. 8, Shimemshan, Southern Song)

阿修羅戦帝釈天物語図局部
——石門山第8号 南宋

千里眼——石门山第2号 北宋

Farsighted God
(No. 2, Shimemshan, Northern Song)

千里眼——石門山第2号 北宋

（第 80 页图片说明）
东岳大忏宝生变相图——石门山第 11 号 南宋

Story of God of Mt. Tai
(No. 11, Shimenshan, Southern Song)

(80 ページの写真説明)
東岳大懺宝生変相図——石門山第 11 号 南宋

独脚五通——石门山第 7 号 南宋

One-legged God
(No. 7, Shimenshan, Southern Song)

独脚五通——石門山第 7 号 南宋

孔雀明王窟──北山第155号 南宋

Cave of Mayurasana, Peacock King
(No.155, Beishan, Northen Song)

孔雀明王窟──北山第155号 南宋

　　窟中孔雀双腿直立，昂首挺胸，展翅开屏，尾羽上翘，栩栩如生。明王趺坐于孔雀背负之莲台上，端庄肃穆。其像精雕细刻，其座大刀阔斧，显得韵律别致。窟壁上遍刻千佛，镌造工整细致，造型玲珑小巧，排列整齐有序，与雄伟的孔雀相互辉映，使其气氛热烈而又主次分明。

　　Mayurasana sits on a lotus-throne borne by a huge peacock which is spreading its wings and turning its beautiful tail upwards like a pillar supporting the roof of the cave. Around the statue much room is left for people to walk. The small Buddha figures are carved exquisitely on the walls of the shrine.

　　窟中に直立した孔雀は、胸を張って両翼と尾羽を広げ、生きているそのものである。明王は孔雀の背中にのせた蓮華座上に端座している。全体はつくりが細密で別に一格の韻律をもつ。窟の四壁にまんべんなく彫られたこじんまりした仏像が、秩序よく並べられ、雄大な孔雀と相い映し合って、主従の位置をはっきりしている。

（第83页图片说明）
千佛──北山第155号 北宋

Thousand Buddhas
(No. 155, Beishan, Northern Song)

(83ページの写真説明)
千仏──北山第155号 北宋

日月观音——北山第136号 南宋

Avalokitesvara with the Sun and Moon
(No.136, Beishan, Southern Song)

日月観音——北山第136号 南宋

文殊菩萨——北山第136号 南宋

Manjusri, Bodhisattva of Wisdom
(No. 136. Beishan, Southern Song)

文殊菩薩——北山第136号 南宋

普贤菩萨——北山第136号 南宋

Samantabhadra, Bodhisattva of Universal Benevolence
(No. 136, Beishan, Southern Song)

玉印观音——北山第136号 南宋

Avalokitesvara with Jade Seal
(No. 136, Beishan, Southern Song)

转轮经藏窟——北山第136号 南宋

Cave for keeping buddhist scriptures
(No. 136, Beishan, Southern Song)

転輪経蔵窟——北山第136号 南宋

　　此窟造像是中国石窟艺术中的精品,被誉为"中国石窟艺术皇冠上的明珠"。其雕造工艺精美绝伦,巧夺天工。刀法准确利落,花簇珠串玲珑剔透,目睹者无不叫绝。其形象、姿态、性格、神情以至衣褶、饰物等,皆耐人寻味。形体有阴阳明暗、方圆曲直之分;线条有长短、粗细、繁简、疏密、刚柔之别,组合变化丰富,有如行云流水,使衣带、褶襞起伏转折,纵横交错,于视觉上使人感受到鲜明的节奏和优美的旋律。绕窟观赏,有步步移、面面观、色色新之妙。其间文殊的开朗自负,普贤的温柔典雅,玉印观音的庄重刚直,日月观音的安详自在,如意珠观音的含蓄稳重,数珠手观音的文静秀美,以及嬉戏儿童的天真烂漫等,皆毫无雷同。雕像既具丰富的"人性",又不失为"仙风道骨"的神。

　　As the splendid stone-carving masterpieces appeared during the late period of the Tang Dynasty and the Five Dynasties (892-960), the figures in cave 136 claim to be a pearl on the crown of Chinese grotto art. They have the features of well-proportioned bodies, exquisitely luxurious garments and distinct characters. For example, Manjusri, the well-learned and eloquent Boddhisattva, was carved into a vigorous figure, sitting on a roaring lion, with a tint of self-conceit. As a match for Manjusri, Samantabhadra was carved as a female Bodhisattva. It possesses the beautiful and healthy features peculiar to an Oriental fairy full of human touch.

　　この窟の造像は中国石窟芸術の逸品と言ってよく、中国石窟芸術の王冠上に綴られた輝く真珠と絶賛されている。造像の数々はつくりが精巧で、彫刻ナイルの捌き方が細密を極め、人物の容貌、姿勢、性格、さらに衣服や飾り物などまでは、玩味させるものばかりである。体形には陰陽明暗、方円曲直の区別があり、線の運用は長短、粗細、繁簡、疎密、剛柔の変化に富でいる。これにより生まれた衣帯の起伏変化から、見る人は鮮明で優美な視覚的メロディーを楽しむことができる。明朗自負の文殊、優しくて典雅な普賢、荘重剛直の玉印観音、ゆったりした日月観音、含蓄で落ち着いた如意珠観音、おとなしくて秀美な数珠手観音、はしゃいでいる子供など造像の数々は同じものがなく、豊かな「人間性」を持っていながらも「仙風道骨」も失っていない。

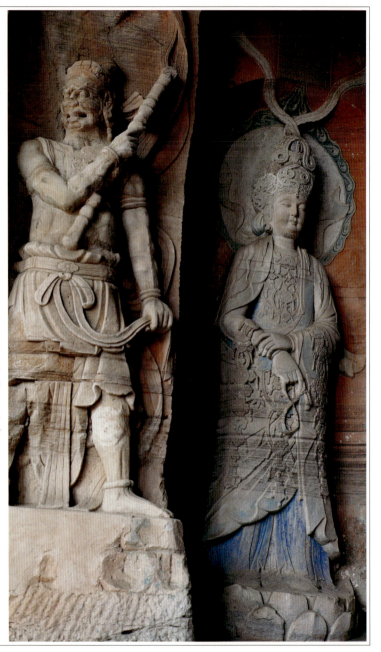

弥勒下生经变相——北山第176号 北宋

Cave of Maitreyavyakarana, Future Buddha
(No. 176, Beishan, Northern Song)

弥勒下生経変相——北山第176号 北宋

地藏菩萨——北山第177号 北宋

Ksitigarbha Bodhisattva
(No. 177, Beishan, Northern Song)

地藏菩薩——北山第177号 北宋

(第89页图片说明)
观无量寿佛经变相——北山第245号 唐末

Sutra of Amitabha and His Pure Land
(No.245, Beishan, Late Tang)

(89ページの写真説明)
観無量寿仏経変相——北山第245号 唐末

　　造像据自《观无量寿佛经》。龛正中刻"西方三圣"，以螺髻金身的阿弥陀佛居中，左为观音，右为大势至菩萨。龛上部展现的是西方极乐盛况，其间八功德池，朱雀翱翔，伎乐起舞，龙凤拽舟，花草争妍。中下部刻"三品九生"。下部和龛外左右侧门柱方框内，刻频婆娑王和韦提希夫人为其太子囚禁，夫人乞佛为说"十六观"等内容。全龛造像表现内容丰富，人物多达五百余尊，小者如豆粒，而无不栩栩如生，充分展示出古代工匠高超的雕刻技艺。

　　This group of stone sculptures were produced in accordance with the Amitayus-Dhana-Sutra. In the centre of this shrine stand the "Three Saints of West". A bust of Amitabha is seated in the middle with Avalokitesvara on his right and Mahasthama on his left. On the uper tier there is a picture which shows the grand scene of the Pure Land of West. "Nine Ranks of Celestials" are carved on the middle and lower tiers. At the east and west corners of the lower tier is the story of 16 meditations of Queen Veidehi. Consisting of more than five hundred statues, the stone sculptures in this shrine are all full of vitality. The magnificent layout and splendid tableau fully reveal the ancient artisans' high skill.

　　造像は『観無量寿仏経』に出典した。窟の真ん中に「三聖」が彫られている。螺髻金身の阿弥陀仏を中央に、左は観音様で、右は大勢至菩薩である。窟の上部は功徳池、飛び舞う朱雀、舞い踊る伎楽、竜舟に乗った鳳凰、美を競う草花など西方極楽世界を描いた場面である。下部は「三品九生」が刻された。下部と龕外左右両側門柱の四角形の枠内に、太子に囚われた頻婆王と韋堤希夫人、夫人が仏に乞いて「十六観」を説くなどの場面が彫られている。造像は内容が豊富で、登場人物が500人を数え、小さいものが豆くらいしかなく、これもどれも生き生きとしていて古代工匠の高い彫刻技芸を示している。

观音像—北山第180号 北宋

The statue of Avalokitesvara
(No. 180, Beishan, Northern Song)

観音像——北山第180号 北宋

(第91页图片说明)
如意轮观音窟——北山第149号 北宋

Cintaanicakra-Avalokitesvara
(No. 149, Beishan, Northern Song)

(91ページの写真説明)
如意輪観音窟——北山第149号 北宋

头像选萃
Selected carved heads
頭像の数々

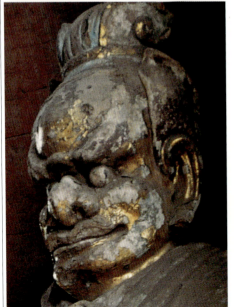